THIS **SACRED CYCLES** JOURNAL

belongs to:

NAME:

_____

EMAIL:

_____

PHONE NUMBER:

_____

If found, please return for the grand reward of deep love & respect

Published in the United States by: Hay House, Inc.: www.hayhouse.com®
Published in Australia by: Hay House Australia Pty. Ltd.: www.hayhouse.com.au
Published in the United Kingdom by: Hay House UK, Ltd.: www.hayhouse.co.uk
Published in India by: Hay House Publishers India: www.hayhouse.co.in

Cover design: Jay Kay & Bryn Starr Best
Interior design: Jay Kay of creative-wannabe.com
Interior illustrations: Jessie White
Jill Pyle author photo: Nora Wendel

Tradepaper ISBN: 978-1-4019-7035-2
10 9 8 7 6 5 4 3 2 1

1st edition, June 2022

THE SACRED CYCLES JOURNAL

Created by the team at

WRITTEN BY

EM DEWEY, @GARDENOFTHEMOON

JILL PYLE, CO-FOUNDER OF GODDESS PROVISIONS

CIDNEY BACHERT, @CIDNEY.ELIZABETH

ILLUSTRATED BY

JESSIE WHITE, @SEEDSOFSPELLS

Find more magic online

🅞 @moonwisdomclub
🅞 @goddessprovisions
🅞 @sacredcyclesoracle

MOONWISDOM.COM
GODDESSPROVISIONS.COM
SACREDCYCLES.COM

HAY HOUSE

Carlsbad, California • New York City
London • Sydney • New Delhi

Listen to Your Body

Contents

Welcome Dear One

Nature beckons you home
The moon illuminates the dark
Spirit's whispers touch your heart
Your body knows where and when to start

Cycles come
And cycles go
As you learn to dance
And find your flow

The guidance you seek
It is always there
As subtle sensation
As divine inspiration

Open to receive
Let the wisdom in
Sing, create, play
Find your divine rhythm

Your path is unfolding
Energies aligning
Follow the signs
And you'll be shining

Cycle
Tracking Guide

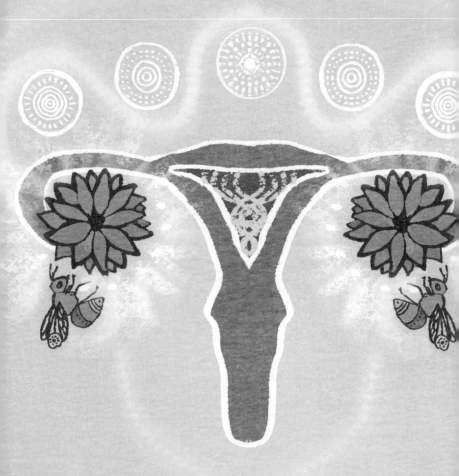

Why Cycle Tracking

Cycle tracking is a practice: the practice of tuning in to your cycle in the name of creating a conversation with your body. It is an act of rebellion, of reclamation, of choosing a radical new way of relating and being in your body. And this new way has the potential to magically shift not only the way you think and feel about your cycles, but even the way your monthly cycles show up in your body.

We All Have Cycles

Cycle tracking is often centered on exploring the monthly menstrual bleeding cycle with the hope of empowering those with this lived experience to reconnect to and even create a new relationship with their inner seasons. This particular exploration is for anyone who menstruates—no matter how you may identify in your gender, sex, or sexuality.

Please know that all humans are cyclical beings. If you are someone who no longer, or has never had, a monthly bleed, the practice of cycle tracking can still be applied to your own life. You can use the cycle tracking charts to observe your patterns more directly to the moon phases, and even the astrological signs the moon moves through. This process can be deeply powerful on both personal and interpersonal levels. Whether cycle tracking directly impacts your own relationship to your cycle, guides you to reflect on your past experiences with menstruating, helps you to better understand those in your life who do bleed, or simply expands your knowledge of the natural world and the way human bodies mirror these cycles—it's all valid and important.

The Grand

Cycles

The Moon, Menstruation & Seasons

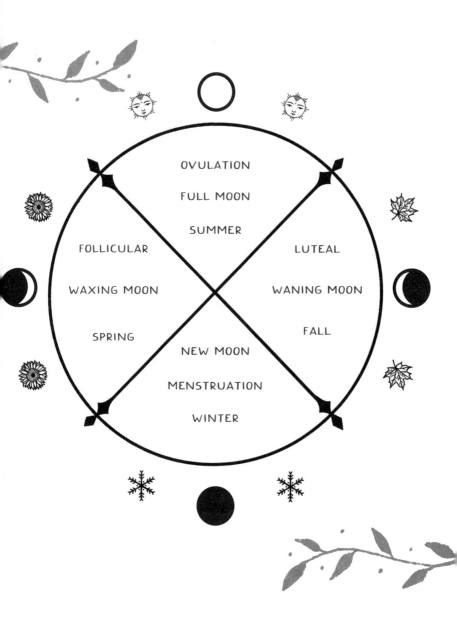

OVULATION

FULL MOON

SUMMER

FOLLICULAR

LUTEAL

WAXING MOON

WANING MOON

SPRING

FALL

NEW MOON

MENSTRUATION

WINTER

How to Get Started

BEGINNING TO TRACK YOUR CYCLE

There are many different ways to track your cycle, whether that be: using a wall calendar, keeping notes in a period app on your phone, or a Cycle Tracking Chart like the ones included within this Sacred Cycles Journal. All are valid ways to approach this experiment, and it's essential to find what works for you.

Whether you are just beginning your cycle tracking journey or are deeply attuned to this practice, this journal is a tangible resource for you. Within each chart, you'll see space to take daily notes as well as where to mark your bleed days (if this applies to you). You'll also find further guidance on how to best record your own observations and reflections. This is the key point of cycle tracking: to document and connect to YOUR personal experience. Through charting our cycles, we become both the scientist and the experiment of our own lives.

Cycle tracking offers us a crash course in learning the language of our bodies. The body's primary form of communication with us is through our physical experiences. So when we tune in to these signals, we begin to open up a dialogue that can lead not only to a more holistic and peaceful experience of our cycles, but also better overall body literacy that can serve us in advocating for our health and well-being.

The longer you continue to track your cycle, the more in tune with your body you will become. You'll soon notice patterns in places that before felt like arbitrary "good" or "bad" days (we'll challenge the notion of labeling experiences as such later on). With the right amount of information and understanding, you may just begin to see the innate wisdom and magic that lies within self-knowledge.

The Four Phases of Wisdom

THE MONTHLY CYCLE & ITS SEASONS

Perhaps the most vital concept to entertain when diving into cycle tracking, is looking at the menstrual cycle as just that—a complete cycle, versus a stand-alone few days/week out of a month. Long before period tracking apps, folks who menstruated recognized the natural connection between the timing of menstruation and the lunar cycle. A continuum of phases that morphed from one right into the next, starting anew but built on the cycle and phase that came before it. In the following section, we'll explore the four main phases of the complete menstrual cycle, while digging deeper into understanding the key lessons and superpowers each holds, as well as the ways each phase is reflected in the natural world around us through its seasonal cycle.

Reminder: The following descriptions of the four main phases of the menstrual cycle and the themes or experiences discussed are each just general ideas and concepts to consider. Please remember that cycle tracking is about understanding YOUR personal experience, and that experience may be quite different than what is described here. True cycle magic arises when you deeply understand your body and then engage in communicating with it through recognizing and working with the mental, emotional, spiritual, and physical sensations that you experience in each phase.

Menstrual Phase

NEW MOON · WINTER

*Introverted * Quiet * Rest * Release*

The cycle begins with the New Moon or days 1–7 of your cycle (or however long you bleed for). This is connected to the lunar phase when the sky is darkest, where the light of the moon seems to have disappeared. Lunar wisdom teaches that this phase connects us to the season of winter—a time of quiet and turning inward.

THE HORMONE STORY

Reflective of the low energy generally felt at this point in the cycle, all three main hormones (estrogen, progesterone, and testosterone) are at their lowest during the time of bleeding. The most profound dip occurs right as bleeding begins, and will gradually start to rise again in the following days of your period. This is why you may start to feel an increase in energy even while you are still bleeding.

MOON MAGIC RITUAL

It is said that during the time one is bleeding that the veil is thinnest and entering the spiritual realms is made most accessible. This is a potent time to work with any divination tools that you are most drawn to, such as tarot or oracle cards. Make space and time for a quiet ritual with your chosen tools, tapping into the psychic energy that is so potent around this phase and asking to be shown the themes and lessons for the cycle that lies ahead.

Mantra

FOR WINTER

*I am allowed deep rest to feed
my soul and align with
my highest good*

Follicular Phase

WAXING MOON - SPRING

Courage ✳ *Curiosity* ✳ *Playful* ✳ *Energized*

After the darkness of the New Moon has passed, the transition to the Waxing Moon phase can feel sweet and playful, like winter turning to springtime. There's a renewed sense of interest in the outside world and a readiness to begin engaging once again. In the New Moon phase, energy was directed inward and toward self-reflection. The Waxing Moon phase begins to call us back out to look at where we'd like to explore next. This is the seed-tending phase of the cycle, where the ideas that were planted during the time of reflection of the New Moon are beginning to take form.

THE HORMONE STORY

As estrogen starts to rise, more energy returns to the body, and the prospect of socializing and being "out in the world" may feel a bit less daunting than during the early days of the cycle. With estrogen's increase, there's an increase in the brain's serotonin, so things may naturally look more optimistic and upbeat!

MOON MAGIC RITUAL

As a dynamic time of renewed energy and excitement, this phase asks for attention and care in cultivating the growing spark within. Use this time to plan healthy meals for the days ahead and move your body in ways that feel deeply invigorating and come from love and playfulness. By tending to the fire in these nourishing ways, it ensures that the magic of the rest of the cycle may also be harnessed.

Mantra

FOR SPRING

I have seen the vision of what my heart desires and move toward it knowing I am worthy

Ovulatory Phase

*Action * Motivated * Productive * Radiant*

This phase is the highest energetic point in the cycle, just like the Full Moon and the summertime season it connects to: big, bright, bold, and wild. Frequently this shows up as a strong sense of confidence and a feeling of certainty as you stand solidly and with determination for what you desire. It likely feels natural to be out in the world and dealing with the many demands of modern-day life. Given the patriarchal structures that we navigate daily and the intense masculine "doing" energy that this phase has associated with it, it's no wonder that this can often feel like the "easy" phase within the cycle, as it is so much more accepted by those around us and the systems we exist within.

THE HORMONE STORY

While ovulation as a biological event is a one-day, one-time-only thing during each cycle, the days surrounding this event (around the midpoint of your cycle) are when estrogen and testosterone are at their highest, giving you a serious boost of "go get 'em" attitude. Just before ovulation, a surge of luteinizing and follicle-stimulating hormones cause one of the mature follicles to release an egg. Biologically, the body has amped up your energy and confidence to peak heights at the same time as when you're most fertile.

MOON MAGIC RITUAL

Planning ahead for this phase can create an opportunity to channel the wild magnetism you are exuding at this time. Make sure to schedule events where you're able to go out and be seen during this phase: a night of dancing, launching a new project, or giving a big speech are ideal during this potent time in your cycle.

Mantra

FOR SUMMER

*My light shines brightest &
inspires others when I am
deeply connected to my truth*

Luteal Phase

*Withdraw * Wind down * Reflection * Discernment*

The same way the bright Full Moon gives way to the decreasing light of the Waning Moon, your energy begins to draw back inward. Here the days of "doing-all-the-things" begin to feel much less appealing, and the energy is instead directed toward embracing a stronger sense of your personal boundaries. It's up to you how these boundaries are expressed. This phase of the cycle can be powerful as you learn to identify what it is that's getting under your skin, and explore the "why" before expressing it outward.

THE HORMONE STORY

Right after estrogen peaks around ovulation, progesterone moves to center stage and starts to take over the show. The follicle that releases the egg during ovulation turns into its own hormone-producing temporary endocrine gland called the corpus luteum. If an egg has been fertilized, progesterone will continue to stay heightened to nurture the fertilized egg (progesterone = pro-gestation). If the egg was not fertilized, progesterone will then begin to fall around 9–11 days after ovulation as the corpus luteum breaks down, leading into the menstruation phase once again.

MOON MAGIC RITUAL

Unplug from the productivity wheel, and explore your connection with unbound creativity. Experimenting with creative energy is a powerful way to work with and monitor the inner critic that can show up as the shadow side of discernment. Whatever means of working with your hands, building, moving your body, or creating—in whatever way you feel called—allow the energy of this phase to channel through you without judgment. By moving this energy through your body, you make space for the next cycle's wisdom to be presented to you.

Mantra

FOR FALL

My truth is both my weapon and my medicine; I wield it with grace and sovereignty

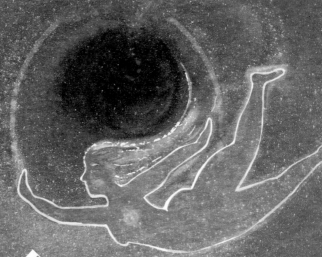

Cyclical

Divination

Lunar Wisdom

MOONTIME BLEEDING INSIGHTS

Cyclical divination, or menstrual divination, is another form of personal magic that you can use to help manifest your best life and attune to your highest self. The divine feminine lies within everyone, but for those who experience monthly bleeding, you are familiar with the ways in which your energy changes over the course of each month. Cyclical divination is similar to any other divination practice; however, you are paying attention to the ways your mind, body, and soul react to those changes within.

There are four general moon cycles that you could become attuned to:

White Moon Cycle - Bleeding with the New Moon

Pink Moon Cycle - Bleeding with the Waxing Moon

Red Moon Cycle - Bleeding with the Full Moon

Purple Moon Cycle - Bleeding with the Waning Moon

Each moon cycle correlates with ovulation and bleeding, and in turn, speaks on several different factors, including where you are in your self-discovery, your spiritual practice, what you could improve upon, and even the energy levels that you may experience during the phases of your moontime. For example, it is recommended that you rest and recover during the menstrual stage of the cycle, but for those who bleed with the New Moon, this is also a great time to plan your next project. Cyclical divination is all about tuning in and using your body's natural abilities to help heighten and expand your emotional and spiritual capacity. It is about harnessing the true power that comes with the ebb and flow of the divine feminine.

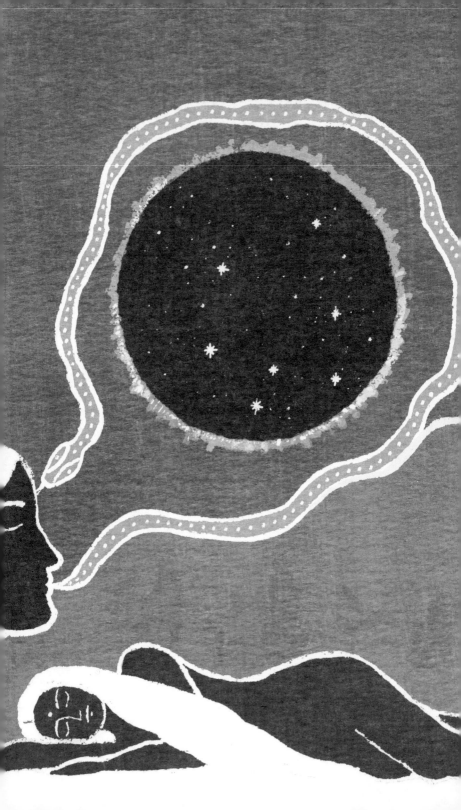

White Moon Cycle

BLEEDING WITH THE NEW MOON

Bleeding with the New Moon creates a connection to your inner mother. This does not mean that it is the time to overly parent yourself and make sure all your chores are done. This is a call to nurture yourself. Self-care is key, so turn inward. What would put a smile on the face of your inner child right now? Whether you are a mother or not, we can all access this nurturing energy and use it to help us heal and grow. Known as the White Moon Cycle, your bleeding begins close to or on the New Moon while your ovulation takes place around the Full Moon. With that in mind, the New Moon is often associated with setting intentions and beginning new projects. As energy levels are typically decreased during menstruation, use this time to reflect and plan instead of beginning a new task or project. What have you learned from your previous projects? How can you plan better? Do you have everything you need to complete it? Use this time to nurture yourself and answer these questions so you can complete your next task efficiently. Once you ovulate with the Full Moon, it will be the perfect time to put your plan into action. Energy will be at its peak, and you have already taken the steps to ensure that you have everything you need to begin.

Pink Moon Cycle

BLEEDING WITH THE WAXING MOON

The Waxing Moon is a call to be playful, lighthearted, and full of life. People with periods have generally been taught that this is a burden, something that sets them back each month. It has been culturally frowned upon to talk about it in public and for many has been a source of embarrassment. As you bleed with the Waxing Moon, toss this idea of burden and embarrassment to the side. Your moon cycle is a symbol of life, fertility, nurturing, and rebirth. This natural process has been occurring for thousands of years—it is what connects us to all cyclical beings around the globe. It is a reminder of change and, like the other natural cycles of the Earth, it is inevitable and refreshing. Your body is shedding so that it can grow anew each month. The Pink Moon Cycle symbolizes growth, and you can't grow if you stay the same. So welcome the change. Like spring, let the energy of the Waxing Moon awaken you from the preceding darkness. Use this time to explore the world around you. Take slow walks in nature, research new places you'd like to visit, and then use the energy of your ovulation during the Waning Moon to wrap up any loose ends before you embark on your next journey.

Red Moon Cycle

✳

BLEEDING WITH THE FULL MOON

A Red Moon Cycle connects you to the powers of the Full Moon. Here lies a deep connection to your sensuality, the divine feminine, and the powerful lineage of those who have come before you. Traditionally, this cycle has been associated with healers, medicine women, and witches and is a great time to send an homage to these great healers and magic makers. Lift yourself up and empower others around you. Let this deeply rooted divine feminine energy flow through you. Bleeding with the Full Moon is the perfect time to get creative (see Moontime Painting p. 35). Sit down with a cup of herbal tea and create a new painting for your home, write a song, or dive into a book. Let the notoriously wild Full Moon energy drive you to color outside the lines. Nothing is too abstract; let your imagination run free. It is also believed that the veil between realms is thinner while you bleed, so now is the perfect time to consult your guides or practice with your divination tools. As you bleed with the Full Moon, recognize that it is at its peak. Use this time to manifest your desires and connect to your spiritual energy. Once the New Moon comes around, use the increased energy from this ovulatory period to help you drive those manifestations into reality.

Purple Moon Cycle

BLEEDING WITH THE WANING MOON

The Purple Moon Cycle presents you with an opportunity each month to explore the depths of your being. This cycle is all about self-discovery, self-awareness, and stepping into your power. Think about yourself for a moment—what you enjoy, what your personality is like. These are all surface level, and while they do define you and help you create relations with others, this is a call to dive deeper. You are a powerful, sovereign, divine being, and it is time to recognize your greatness. As we move through each lifetime, we learn lessons that help us align with our highest self. See if you notice any recurring themes of distress during this time, whether it be your job, a relationship, or something in your home. How can this issue be resolved? Is what's bothering you truly serving you and your soul's purpose, or is it standing in your way? Bleeding with the Waning Moon is an opportunity to connect to your soul's purpose and ask the divine the questions that may have been weighing on you. The answers are within you. Meditation and journaling are two tools that can be helpful to you during this time. Once ovulation begins with the Waxing Moon, you can take your new findings out into the world and explore them further.

Bleeding Rituals

Honoring Your Bleeding

Through your cycle tracking practice, you are actively rewriting the narrative around periods. There is a long history of shame and stigma that has negatively impacted people with periods, whether it was needing to separate from others during bleeding or being thought of as impure. As we enter into a new age of understanding, it is time to shed the layers of this stigma. Stand proud in your ability to bleed and grow each month. Aside from getting more comfortable with your monthly cycle, we have included a few rituals that you can practice to help embrace your moontime and embody the energy of the divine feminine.

Moontime Painting

✳

WHAT YOU'LL NEED

Canvas or paper
Paintbrushes
Mason jar or covered bowl
Period blood
Items to set the ambiance

HOW TO CREATE YOUR MASTERPIECE

Painting with your own period blood may feel daunting at first, but we are here to release the stigma around all things menstrual. You'll begin by collecting menstrual blood by using a period cup, disc, or by free bleeding. This way, you can collect more of this sacred material with ease. Pour the contents into a covered bowl or mason jar and store in the fridge until you are ready to use it. Once you have selected what you'll be painting on, whether it's canvas, cloth, or paper, and you have gathered enough blood, then the painting process can begin. This is a ritual, so prepare the space as you would if you were practicing anything else. Cleanse the space, light your favorite candles or incense, or brew a cup of tea. Maybe even decorate with a bouquet of fresh flowers to tap into the divine feminine energy of nature. When you feel ready, set up your painting materials and begin. Paint whatever calls to you or feels right at that moment. There is no right or wrong way to create, especially when you are creating with a true piece of yourself.

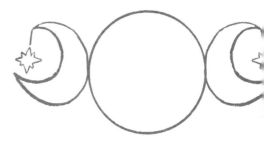

Blessed Blooms

WHAT YOU'LL NEED

Mason jar or covered bowl
Period blood
Water
A garden or plants

HOW TO WATER THE EARTH

If you've ever had a vegetable or herb garden, or even indoor plants, you know how rewarding it is to see them thrive and produce beautiful blooms or voluptuous veggies. This ritual is an offering to the Earth and your plants. We take so much from the Earth, so it only makes sense to give back to it. You'll begin by collecting your menstrual blood using a period cup, disc, or free bleeding. Store this in a mason jar or covered bowl in the fridge until you are ready to use it. When you are ready, you'll want to dilute your period blood with water. This is because the salt content of the blood will be too high for your plants. The best way to dilute it is one part blood to nine parts water (i.e. 1 Tbsp blood and 9 Tbsp water). With your mixture in hand, close your eyes and say a few words of gratitude. Give thanks to your body and its cyclical processes, and to the Earth and the food it provides us. Then set an intention for what you would like the Earth to receive from this offering. When you feel that the intention has been set, begin to water your plants with the mixture. Note: It is recommended to do this with outdoor plants and herbs rather than house plants, as house plants may not react the same way.

Sacred Cycles Facial

WHAT YOU'LL NEED

Mason jar or covered bowl
Period blood
Optional: Facial Brush

HOW TO CREATE YOUR FACIAL

It has been reported that menstrual blood has stem cells, which can help to reduce acne and acne scarring. In this ritual, you will be collecting your menstrual blood to use as a facial. Please note that this is not recommended if you are on any type of hormonal birth control, as you would be adding additional hormones to the face and potentially creating more acne. To begin, collect the first day of your monthly cycle by using a period cup, disc, or free bleeding. Pour in a mason jar or bowl to use immediately. This covers two things, the first being that you won't be putting a cold mixture on your face that could close up the pores. The second is that you will be using fresh blood rather than the end of the cycle. When you are ready to begin, cleanse your face using your favorite natural cleanser and warm water. Then, use either your clean hands or a facial brush to apply the blood evenly around the face, avoiding the eyes and the mouth. Let it sit for 15–20 minutes. During this time, meditate, practice some light yoga, or pull from your favorite tarot deck. Every moment can be practiced mindfully. When your time is up, rinse your face off with lukewarm water or cleanse again if you prefer. Notice how your skin looks at that moment. Continue with your chosen skincare routine and moisturize.

Womb-To-Earth Free Bleeding

✳

WHAT YOU'LL NEED

A patch of Earth
A few hours of your day
Your favorite book and drink

HOW TO FREE BLEED

To begin this ritual, find an area of outdoor space where you can sit in peace and privacy. Prepare the space by cleansing it, creating an offering for the Earth, or sitting in meditation. When you are in your moontime, gather some pillows or blankets and set them out around this area so you can be comfortable. Gather a few of your other favorite items, whether that's a book or magazine, tea, or your pet. You will be spending some time outdoors, so if you can grab what you'll need for an hour or two, that would be best. Set the items up around you so that you'll be able to bleed cleanly onto the Earth. Enjoy spending quiet time outdoors. Listen with intention to the birds, the wind whistling through the trees. Spend time meditating and giving thanks for your body's cycles and being able to give back to the Earth in this way. The goal of this ritual is to connect with the Earth, to connect with what creates so much for us. It establishes a sense of grounding and completes this cycle of rebirth. It is also a simple way to break the stigma around periods—just being able to sit outside in peace and not have to worry about running to change a tampon or stressing about the day. Just a human being in nature, nothing more.

Red Tent Celebration

WHAT YOU'LL NEED

Delectable food and drink
Red items or decorations
A few of your favorite people

HOW TO CELEBRATE

This ritual is a celebration and really connects to the roots of ancient moontime practices. Here is a call to celebrate what naturally occurs every month. Rather than dread it, celebrate it! Turn it into another reason to spend time with your friends and eat some of your favorite foods. The idea stems from the historical context of women in tribal settings moving away from others during their monthly cycle to bleed together. To begin, you'll want to clean and cleanse your space. After all, you are hosting a party! When you are finished, gather red items from around the home or head out to your local thrift store and see what you can find. These can be red pillows, blankets, serving dishes, or candles. The goal is to create an inviting space that channels divine feminine energy. Food and drinks are next, and you'll want to make sure you don't skimp. Grab your favorites and encourage your friends to do the same. When the date has come, use this as a time to relax and enjoy the company of those you love. Play games, pull cards for each other or even practice some light yoga together. This celebration is about honoring the divine feminine in everyone.

Go

Within

Triple Goddess Oracle Spread

Maiden   Mother   Crone

INSTRUCTIONS

This spread can help you channel divine feminine energy and call upon each stage of its wisdom. We all embody the stages of the Triple Goddess as we grow and experience life. How can we call upon that learning to help us in the process? Safely lighting a floral candle or incense can help set the scene for this spread and channel divine feminine energy. Begin in a comfortable position, preferably seated, and close your eyes. Hold the cards in your hands and set your intention with this spread in mind. Once you feel like the intention has been set within the cards, open your eyes, and begin to shuffle. If a card falls out, pick that one and place it in a row. Continue with the other two cards. If shuffling is difficult for you, lay the cards out in a line and run your hand over them. Pick the three cards that call to you that way.

REFLECTION

1. **Maiden:** *How can I explore my spirituality in new ways?*

2. **Mother:** *How can I nurture myself and my inner child?*

3. **Crone:** *In what ways can I continue to grow?*

Monthly Moontime Spread

| New Moon | Waxing Moon | Full Moon | Waning Moon |

INSTRUCTIONS

Similar to pulling cards for the month ahead, this Monthly Moontime Spread can help you plan for your moon cycle to come. How should you relax during the New Moon? What can you work on during the Waxing Moon? Begin in a comfortable position, preferably seated, and close your eyes. Hold the cards in your hands and set your intention with this spread in mind. Once you feel like the intention has been set within the cards, open your eyes and begin to shuffle. If a card falls out, pick that one and place it in a row. Continue with the other three cards. If shuffling is difficult for you, lay the cards out in a line and run your hand over them. Pick the four cards that call to you that way.

REFLECTION

1. New Moon: *How can I turn inward and nurture my soul?*

2. Waxing Moon: *What should I focus on in the month to come?*

3. Full Moon: *What am I manifesting this cycle?*

4. Waning Moon: *How can I experiment creatively?*

Self-Care & Your Cycle

SELF-CARE SUGGESTIONS BASED ON EACH PHASE OF THE MENSTRUAL & LUNAR CYCLES

NEW MOON - MENSTRUATION

Journal and reflect on the past month to acknowledge what worked and what felt out of alignment. Then set your intentions for visualizing how you hope to see the next cycle manifest.

WAXING MOON - FOLLICULAR

Explore something new (a hobby, new social group or relationship, a skill you'd like to build)—perhaps inviting a friend or partner along for the new adventure.

FULL MOON - OVULATION

Embrace your ability to manifest just about anything right now by asking for what you truly want. Your confidence and self-worth are fully tuned in and activated during this phase.

WANING MOON - LUTEAL

Wrap up any loose ends at this time that would prevent you from being able to take a bit of time and space for yourself before heading into the quiet of the New Moon or menstruation phase.

A Sacred Offering

Here you hold a dream
A hope and a wish
But also a knowing

A knowing that you
Already have
Already are
All that you need

This body
These cycles
This Earth
These seasons

There is no mistake
No possible error
In the way you were designed
And the way you are experiencing
yourself right now

A Blessing
& Prayer

This is a prayer
And a reminder
That all timing
Is good timing

So if ever you doubt the perfection of
Your dynamic body and your fluid emotions
Your mercurial mind and your
consistent inconsistencies
Return to nature

To the Divine's reminder
Made manifest upon this Earth for you
Through seasons and cycles
The proof that nothing was ever meant
to stay the same

And please, dear one, remember
There is a holy power
In coming home
To this body and your Sacred Cycles

Cycle Tracking Charts

Throughout the rest of this journal you'll find a blank version of the chart like the one (on) the following page. Each circular calendar shows the days and dates with space for note taking as well as a droplet symbol for each day, which can be filled in on the da(ys) you bleed.

At night before going to sleep, reflect on the day's experience. This is a daily practice, s(o) ensuring that your journal is easily accessible is key! In the corresponding day's slice of the wheel, use either symbols or words to describe your experience (some suggestions have been made below, but feel free to get creative!). Here are some themes with a fe(w) potential descriptive words that might be helpful to reflect upon:

- Energy levels: low, high, sleepy, wired
- Moods or Feelings: excited, inspired, quiet, anxious, depressed, optimistic, frustrated
- Physical body: achey, energized, strong, weak, cramps
- Socializing: extroverted (wanting to be around people), introverted (preferring to be alon(e))
- Work: trouble focusing, highly motivated, creative, uninspired, team oriented, independen(t)
- Sexual energy and/or days you were sexually active

All of these themes and words are merely suggestions however, so please make sure you are taking note of the things that stand out and are important to you.

As you continue this practice over the coming months, you may be surprised to notice certain patterns that you were unaware of before. Regardless of what you find, know th(at) this experience is specific to you and that is the magic of it. The self-awareness that this practice brings can lead to a deeper more positive connection to your body, your ment(al) health, and even to the relationships you have with those around you.

Cycle Tracking Chart Example

JANUARY 2022

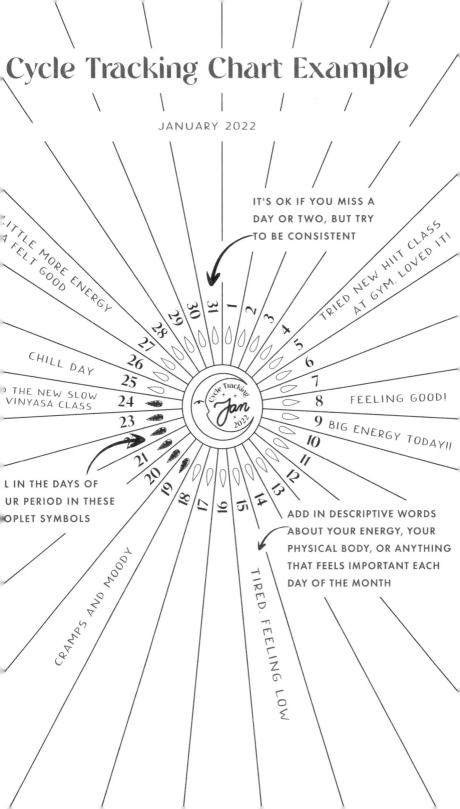

IT'S OK IF YOU MISS A
DAY OR TWO, BUT TRY
TO BE CONSISTENT

TRIED NEW HIIT CLASS
AT GYM, LOVED IT!

...ITTLE MORE ENERGY
...A FELT GOOD

CHILL DAY

... THE NEW SLOW
VINYASA CLASS

FEELING GOOD!

BIG ENERGY TODAY!!

...L IN THE DAYS OF
...UR PERIOD IN THESE
...OPLET SYMBOLS

ADD IN DESCRIPTIVE WORDS
ABOUT YOUR ENERGY, YOUR
PHYSICAL BODY, OR ANYTHING
THAT FEELS IMPORTANT EACH
DAY OF THE MONTH

CRAMPS AND MOODY

TIRED, FEELING LOW

Cycle Tracking
Jan
2022

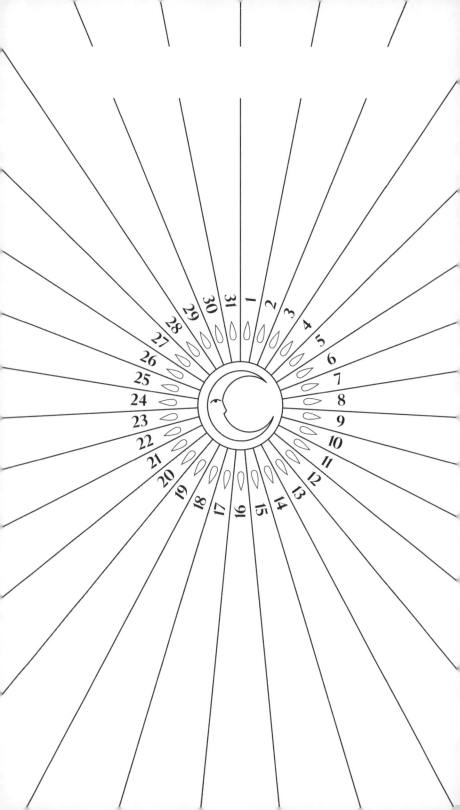

Honor Your Cycle

CYCLE MONTH/YEAR: _____

OVERALL VIBE OF THIS CYCLE: _____

NUMBER OF DAYS BLEEDING: _____

ONE WORD TO DESCRIBE EACH PHASE

MENSTRUATION: _____ FOLLICULAR: _____

OVULATION: _____ LUTEAL: _____

FLOW

Describe your flow for this monthly cycle.

_____

_____

_____

MOON PHASE

What phase was the moon in on the first day of your cycle?

_____

_____

Bleeding Ritual

How did you honor your cycle?

_____

_____

_____

My Cycle Reflections

CYCLE MONTH/YEAR:_____

_____

_____

_____

_____

_____

_____

_____

_____

_____

_____

_____

_____

_____

_____

_____

_____

_____

_____

_____

_____

_____

_____

Journal Prompt For This Cycle:

What are a few ways that you can honor your natural cycles this month?

_____

_____

_____

_____

_____

_____

_____

_____

_____

_____

_____

_____

_____

_____

_____

_____

_____

_____

_____

_____

_____

_____

_____

_____

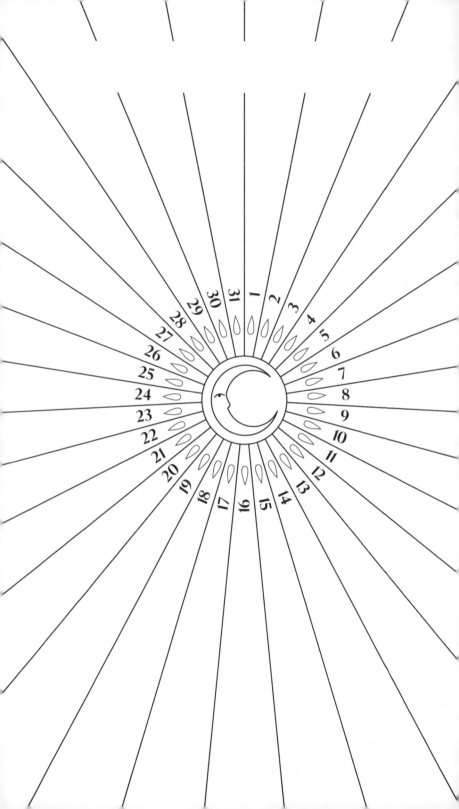

Honor Your Cycle

CYCLE MONTH/YEAR: _____

OVERALL VIBE OF THIS CYCLE: _____

NUMBER OF DAYS BLEEDING: _____

ONE WORD TO DESCRIBE EACH PHASE

MENSTRUATION: _____ FOLLICULAR: _____

OVULATION: _____ LUTEAL: _____

FLOW

Describe your flow for this monthly cycle.

_____

_____

_____

MOON PHASE

What phase was the moon in on the first day of your cycle?

_____

_____

Bleeding Ritual

How did you honor your cycle?

_____

_____

_____

My Cycle Reflections

CYCLE MONTH/YEAR:_____

_____
_____
_____
_____
_____
_____
_____
_____
_____
_____
_____
_____
_____
_____
_____
_____
_____
_____
_____
_____
_____
_____
_____

Journal Prompt For This Cycle:

Think about the other cycles you experience in life. What wisdom do those cycles offer?

_____

_____

_____

_____

_____

_____

_____

_____

_____

_____

_____

_____

_____

_____

_____

_____

_____

_____

_____

_____

_____

_____

_____

_____

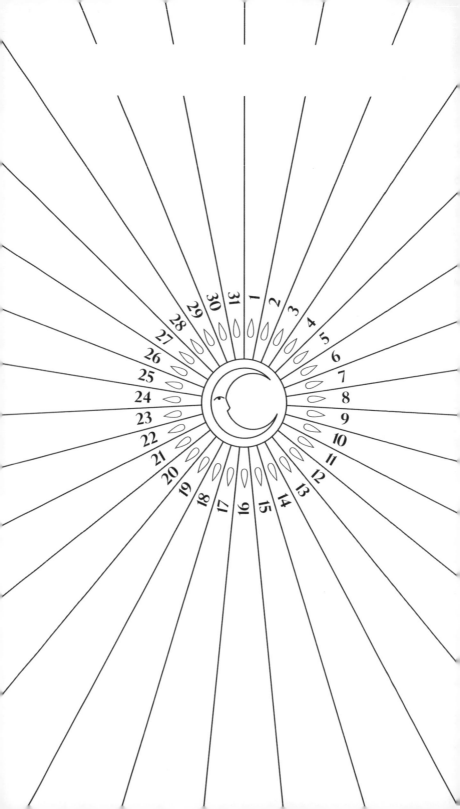

Honor Your Cycle

CYCLE MONTH/YEAR: _____

OVERALL VIBE OF THIS CYCLE: _____

NUMBER OF DAYS BLEEDING: _____

ONE WORD TO DESCRIBE EACH PHASE

MENSTRUATION: _____   FOLLICULAR: _____

OVULATION: _____   LUTEAL: _____

FLOW

Describe your flow for this monthly cycle.

_____

_____

_____

MOON PHASE

What phase was the moon in on the first day of your cycle?

_____

_____

Bleeding Ritual

How did you honor your cycle?

_____

_____

_____

My Cycle Reflections

CYCLE MONTH/YEAR:_____

_____
_____
_____
_____
_____
_____
_____
_____
_____
_____
_____
_____
_____
_____
_____
_____
_____
_____
_____
_____
_____
_____
_____
_____

Journal Prompt For This Cycle:

What foods do you crave before your menstruation?

_____

_____

_____

_____

_____

_____

_____

_____

_____

_____

_____

_____

_____

_____

_____

_____

_____

_____

_____

_____

_____

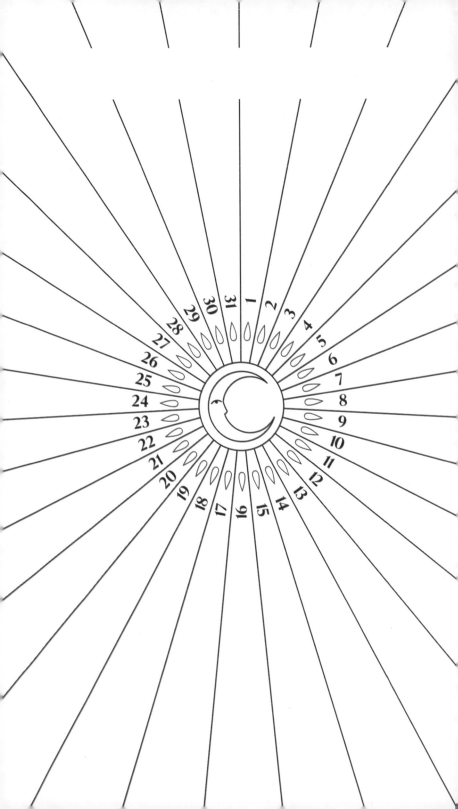

Honor Your Cycle

CYCLE MONTH/YEAR: _____

OVERALL VIBE OF THIS CYCLE: _____

NUMBER OF DAYS BLEEDING: _____

ONE WORD TO DESCRIBE EACH PHASE

MENSTRUATION: _____   FOLLICULAR: _____

OVULATION: _____   LUTEAL: _____

FLOW

Describe your flow for this monthly cycle.

_____

_____

_____

MOON PHASE

What phase was the moon in on the first day of your cycle?

_____

_____

Bleeding Ritual

How did you honor your cycle?

_____

_____

_____

My Cycle Reflections

CYCLE MONTH/YEAR:_____

_____
_____
_____
_____
_____
_____
_____
_____
_____
_____
_____
_____
_____
_____
_____
_____
_____
_____
_____
_____
_____
_____
_____
_____

Journal Prompt For This Cycle:

What moon phase did you bleed with this month?
Did you notice any similarities to the descriptions on pages 23–31?

_____

_____

_____

_____

_____

_____

_____

_____

_____

_____

_____

_____

_____

_____

_____

_____

_____

_____

_____

_____

_____

_____

_____

_____

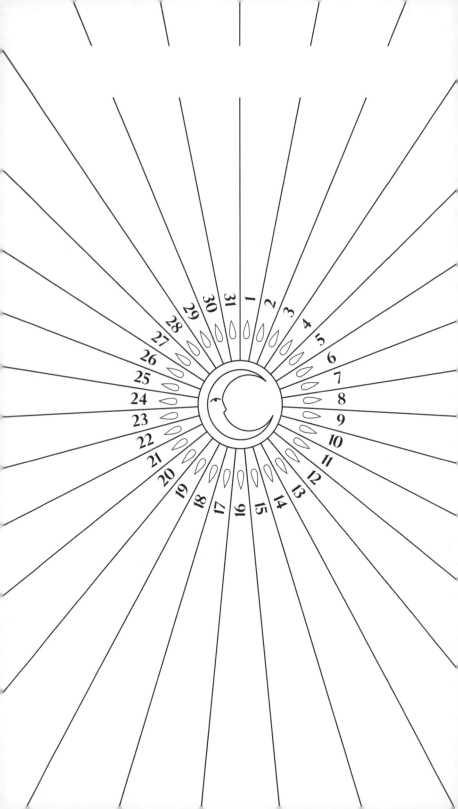

Honor Your Cycle

CYCLE MONTH/YEAR: _____

OVERALL VIBE OF THIS CYCLE: _____

NUMBER OF DAYS BLEEDING: _____

ONE WORD TO DESCRIBE EACH PHASE

MENSTRUATION: _____   FOLLICULAR: _____

OVULATION: _____   LUTEAL: _____

FLOW

Describe your flow for this monthly cycle.

_____

_____

_____

MOON PHASE

What phase was the moon in on the first day of your cycle?

_____

_____

Bleeding Ritual

How did you honor your cycle?

_____

_____

_____

My Cycle Reflections

CYCLE MONTH/YEAR:_____

_____

_____

_____

_____

_____

_____

_____

_____

_____

_____

_____

_____

_____

_____

_____

_____

_____

_____

_____

_____

_____

_____

_____

Journal Prompt For This Cycle:

How does tracking your monthly cycle make you feel?

_____

_____

_____

_____

_____

_____

_____

_____

_____

_____

_____

_____

_____

_____

_____

_____

_____

_____

_____

_____

_____

_____

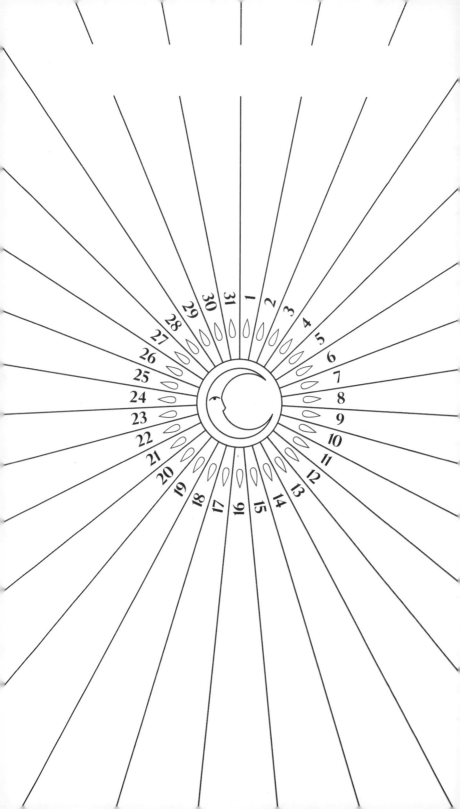

Honor Your Cycle

CYCLE MONTH/YEAR: _____

OVERALL VIBE OF THIS CYCLE: _____

NUMBER OF DAYS BLEEDING: _____

ONE WORD TO DESCRIBE EACH PHASE

MENSTRUATION: _____   FOLLICULAR: _____

OVULATION: _____   LUTEAL: _____

FLOW

Describe your flow for this monthly cycle.

_____

_____

_____

MOON PHASE

What phase was the moon in on the first day of your cycle?

_____

_____

Bleeding Ritual

How did you honor your cycle?

_____

_____

_____

My Cycle Reflections

CYCLE MONTH/YEAR:_____

_____

_____

_____

_____

_____

_____

_____

_____

_____

_____

_____

_____

_____

_____

_____

_____

_____

_____

_____

_____

_____

_____

_____

Journal Prompt For This Cycle:

Write a list of all the things you love about your body.

_____

_____

_____

_____

_____

_____

_____

_____

_____

_____

_____

_____

_____

_____

_____

_____

_____

_____

_____

_____

_____

_____

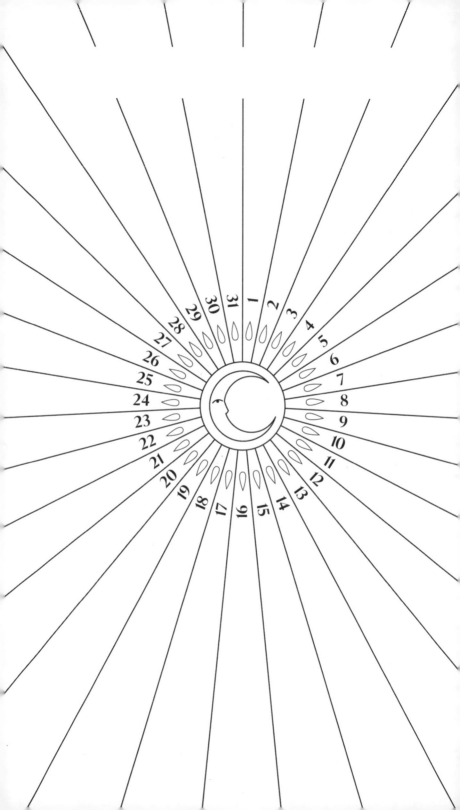

Honor Your Cycle

CYCLE MONTH/YEAR: _____

OVERALL VIBE OF THIS CYCLE: _____

NUMBER OF DAYS BLEEDING: _____

ONE WORD TO DESCRIBE EACH PHASE

MENSTRUATION: _____   FOLLICULAR: _____

OVULATION: _____   LUTEAL: _____

FLOW

Describe your flow for this monthly cycle.

_____

_____

_____

MOON PHASE

What phase was the moon in on the first day of your cycle?

_____

_____

Bleeding Ritual

How did you honor your cycle?

_____

_____

_____

My Cycle Reflections

CYCLE MONTH/YEAR:_____

_____

_____

_____

_____

_____

_____

_____

_____

_____

_____

_____

_____

_____

_____

_____

_____

_____

_____

_____

_____

_____

Journal Prompt For This Cycle:

Describe your perfect relaxation routine. How can you apply this during your monthly cycle?

_____

_____

_____

_____

_____

_____

_____

_____

_____

_____

_____

_____

_____

_____

_____

_____

_____

_____

_____

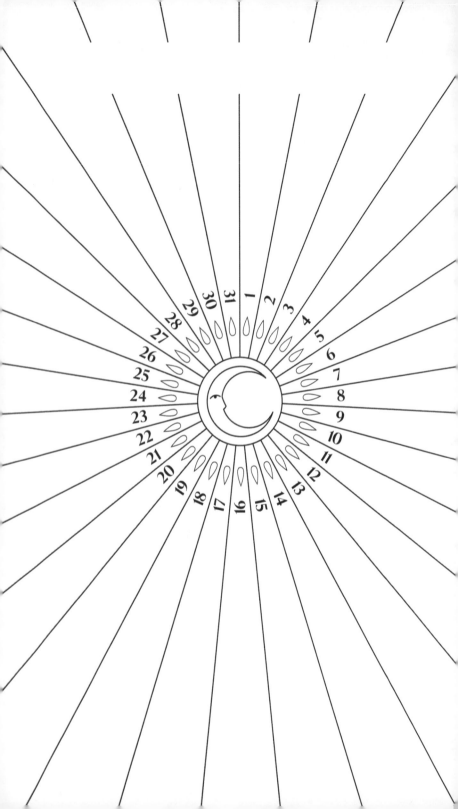

Honor Your Cycle

CYCLE MONTH/YEAR: _____

OVERALL VIBE OF THIS CYCLE: _____

NUMBER OF DAYS BLEEDING: _____

ONE WORD TO DESCRIBE EACH PHASE

MENSTRUATION: _____ FOLLICULAR: _____

OVULATION: _____ LUTEAL: _____

FLOW

Describe your flow for this monthly cycle.

_____

_____

_____

MOON PHASE

What phase was the moon in on the first day of your cycle?

_____

_____

Bleeding Ritual

How did you honor your cycle?

_____

_____

_____

My Cycle Reflections

CYCLE MONTH/YEAR:_____

_____
_____
_____
_____
_____
_____
_____
_____
_____
_____
_____
_____
_____
_____
_____
_____
_____
_____
_____
_____
_____
_____
_____
_____
_____

Journal Prompt For This Cycle:

What kind of bleeding ritual intrigues you the most, and why are you drawn to it?

_____

_____

_____

_____

_____

_____

_____

_____

_____

_____

_____

_____

_____

_____

_____

_____

_____

_____

_____

_____

_____

_____

_____

_____

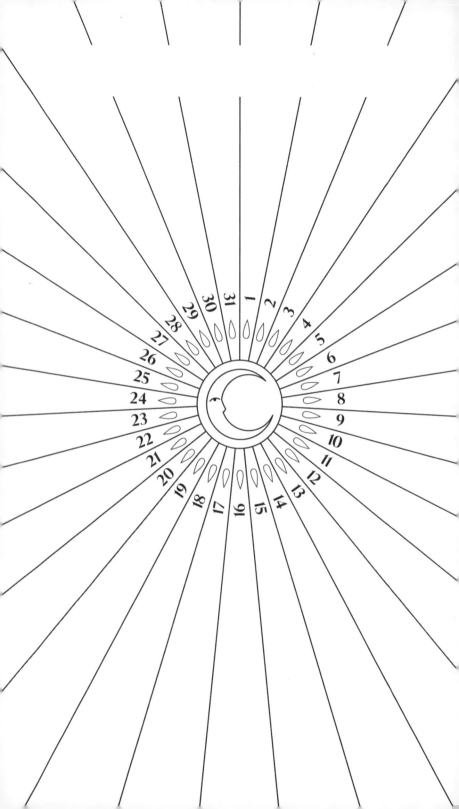

Honor Your Cycle

CYCLE MONTH/YEAR: _____

OVERALL VIBE OF THIS CYCLE: _____

NUMBER OF DAYS BLEEDING: _____

ONE WORD TO DESCRIBE EACH PHASE

MENSTRUATION: _____   FOLLICULAR: _____

OVULATION: _____   LUTEAL: _____

FLOW

Describe your flow for this monthly cycle.

_____

_____

_____

MOON PHASE

What phase was the moon in on the first day of your cycle?

_____

_____

Bleeding Ritual

How did you honor your cycle?

_____

_____

_____

My Cycle Reflections

CYCLE MONTH/YEAR:

Journal Prompt For This Cycle:

What physical symptoms are you starting to notice about different phases of your cycle?

_____

_____

_____

_____

_____

_____

_____

_____

_____

_____

_____

_____

_____

_____

_____

_____

_____

_____

_____

_____

_____

_____

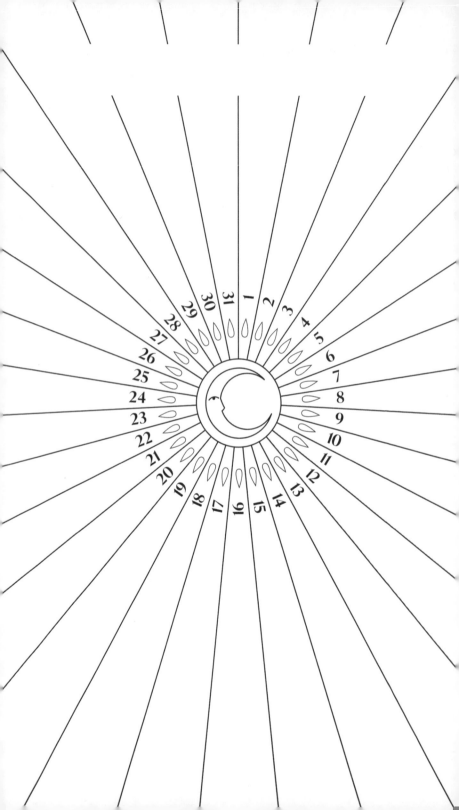

Honor Your Cycle

CYCLE MONTH/YEAR: _____

OVERALL VIBE OF THIS CYCLE: _____

NUMBER OF DAYS BLEEDING: _____

ONE WORD TO DESCRIBE EACH PHASE

MENSTRUATION: _____   FOLLICULAR: _____

OVULATION: _____   LUTEAL: _____

FLOW

Describe your flow for this monthly cycle.

_____

_____

_____

MOON PHASE

What phase was the moon in on the first day of your cycle?

_____

_____

Bleeding Ritual

How did you honor your cycle?

_____

_____

_____

My Cycle Reflections

CYCLE MONTH/YEAR:_____

_____

_____

_____

_____

_____

_____

_____

_____

_____

_____

_____

_____

_____

_____

_____

_____

_____

_____

_____

_____

_____

_____

Journal Prompt For This Cycle:

In which phase of your cycle do you feel most comfortable and relaxed?
And which phase feels more intense or sensitive?

_____

_____

_____

_____

_____

_____

_____

_____

_____

_____

_____

_____

_____

_____

_____

_____

_____

_____

_____

_____

_____

_____

_____

_____

_____

_____

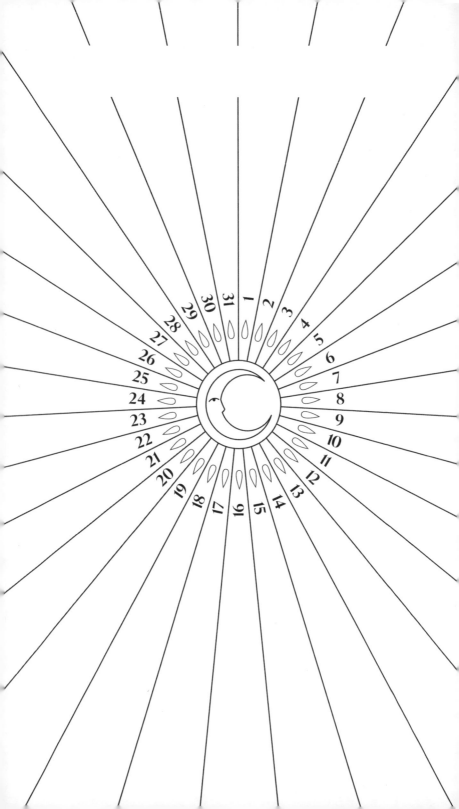

Honor Your Cycle

CYCLE MONTH/YEAR: _____

OVERALL VIBE OF THIS CYCLE: _____

NUMBER OF DAYS BLEEDING: _____

ONE WORD TO DESCRIBE EACH PHASE

MENSTRUATION: _____   FOLLICULAR: _____

OVULATION: _____   LUTEAL: _____

FLOW

Describe your flow for this monthly cycle.

_____

_____

_____

MOON PHASE

What phase was the moon in on the first day of your cycle?

_____

_____

Bleeding Ritual

How did you honor your cycle?

_____

_____

_____

My Cycle Reflections

CYCLE MONTH/YEAR:_____

_____

_____

_____

_____

_____

_____

_____

_____

_____

_____

_____

_____

_____

_____

_____

_____

_____

_____

_____

_____

_____

_____

_____

Journal Prompt For This Cycle:

What changes do you notice as you approach your monthly cycle?
Are they consistent, or do they change throughout the year?

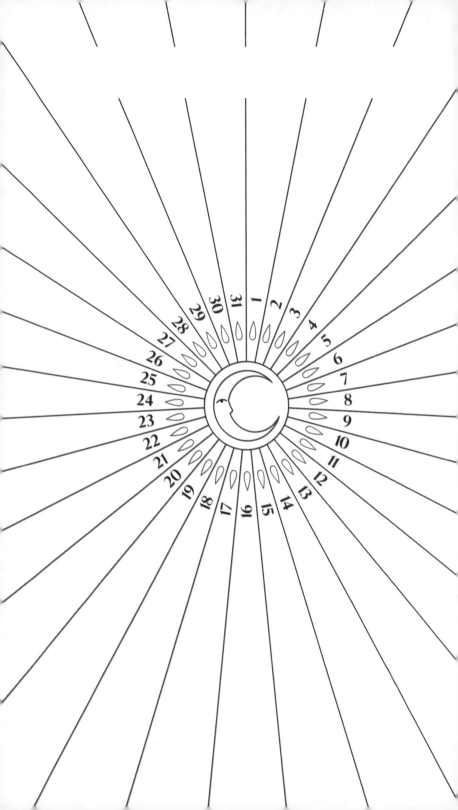

Honor Your Cycle

CYCLE MONTH/YEAR: _____

OVERALL VIBE OF THIS CYCLE: _____

NUMBER OF DAYS BLEEDING: _____

ONE WORD TO DESCRIBE EACH PHASE

MENSTRUATION: _____ FOLLICULAR: _____

OVULATION: _____ LUTEAL: _____

FLOW

Describe your flow for this monthly cycle.

_____

_____

_____

MOON PHASE

What phase was the moon in on the first day of your cycle?

_____

_____

Bleeding Ritual

How did you honor your cycle?

_____

_____

_____

My Cycle Reflections

CYCLE MONTH/YEAR:_____

_____

_____

_____

_____

_____

_____

_____

_____

_____

_____

_____

_____

_____

_____

_____

_____

_____

_____

_____

_____

_____

_____

_____

Journal Prompt For This Cycle:

In what ways does your monthly cycle empower you?

_____

_____

_____

_____

_____

_____

_____

_____

_____

_____

_____

_____

_____

_____

_____

_____

_____

_____

_____

_____

_____

_____

_____

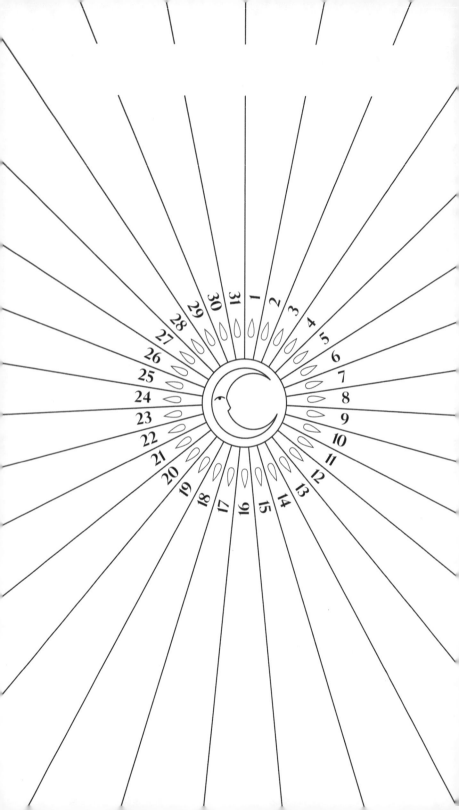

Honor Your Cycle

CYCLE MONTH/YEAR: _____

OVERALL VIBE OF THIS CYCLE: _____

NUMBER OF DAYS BLEEDING: _____

ONE WORD TO DESCRIBE EACH PHASE

MENSTRUATION: _____ FOLLICULAR: _____

OVULATION: _____ LUTEAL: _____

FLOW

Describe your flow for this monthly cycle.

_____

_____

_____

MOON PHASE

What phase was the moon in on the first day of your cycle?

_____

_____

Bleeding Ritual

How did you honor your cycle?

_____

_____

_____

My Cycle Reflections

CYCLE MONTH/YEAR:_____

_____

_____

_____

_____

_____

_____

_____

_____

_____

_____

_____

_____

_____

_____

_____

_____

_____

_____

_____

_____

_____

Journal Prompt For This Cycle:

What has tracking your monthly cycle taught you?

_____

_____

_____

_____

_____

_____

_____

_____

_____

_____

_____

_____

_____

_____

_____

_____

_____

_____

_____

_____

_____

2022 New & Full Moon Dates

New Moon in Capricorn **January 2 @ 10:33 AM PST**

Full Moon in Cancer **January 17 @ 3:48 PM PST**

New Moon in Aquarius **January 31 @ 9:45 PM PST**

Full Moon in Leo **February 16 @ 8:56 AM PST**

New Moon in Pisces **March 2 @ 9:34 AM PST**

Full Moon in Virgo **March 18 @ 12:17 AM PDT**

New Moon in Aries **March 31 @ 11:24 PM PDT**

Full Moon in Libra **April 16 @ 11:54 AM PDT**

New Moon in Taurus **April 30 @ 1:27 PM PDT**

Full Moon in Scorpio **May 15 @ 9:12 PM PDT**

New Moon in Gemini **May 30 @ 4:30 AM PDT**

Full Moon in Sagittarius **June 14 @ 4:51 AM PDT**

New Moon in Cancer **June 28 @ 7:52 PM PDT**

Full Moon in Capricorn **July 13 @ 11:37 AM PDT**

New Moon in Leo **July 28 @ 10:54 AM PDT**

Full Moon in Aquarius **August 11 @ 6:35 PM PDT**

New Moon in Virgo **August 27 @ 1:16 AM PDT**

Full Moon in Pisces **September 10 @ 2:58 AM PDT**

New Moon in Libra **September 25 @ 2:54 PM PDT**

Full Moon in Aries **October 9 @ 1:54 PM PDT**

New Moon in Scorpio **October 25 @ 3:48 AM PDT**

Full Moon in Taurus **November 8 @ 3:00 AM PST**

New Moon in Sagittarius **November 23 @ 2:57 PM PST**

Full Moon in Gemini **December 7 @ 8:07 PM PST**

New Moon in Capricorn **December 23 @ 2:16 AM PST**

2023 New & Full Moon Dates

Full Moon in Cancer **January 6 @ 3:07 PM PST**

New Moon in Aquarius **January 21 @ 12:53 PM PST**

Full Moon in Leo **February 5 @ 10:28 AM PST**

New Moon in Pisces **February 19 @ 11:05 PM PST**

Full Moon in Virgo **March 7 @ 4:40 AM PST**

New Moon in Aries **March 21 @ 10:22 AM PDT**

Full Moon in Libra **April 5 @ 9:34 PM PDT**

New Moon in Aries **April 19 @ 9:12 PM PDT**

Full Moon in Scorpio **May 5 @ 10:33 AM PDT**

New Moon in Taurus **May 19 @ 8:53 AM PDT**

Full Moon in Sagittarius **June 3 @ 8:41 PM PDT**

New Moon in Gemini **June 17 @ 9:36 PM PDT**

Full Moon in Capricorn **July 3 @ 4:38 AM PDT**

New Moon in Cancer **July 17 @ 11:31 AM PDT**

Full Moon in Aquarius **August 1 @ 11:31 AM PDT**

New Moon in Leo **August 16 @ 2:37 AM PDT**

Full Moon in Pisces **August 30 @ 6:35 PM PDT**

New Moon in Virgo **September 14 @ 6:39 PM PDT**

Full Moon in Aries **September 29 @ 2:57 AM PDT**

New Moon in Libra **October 14 @ 10:54 AM PDT**

Full Moon in Taurus **October 28 @ 1:23 PM PDT**

New Moon in Scorpio **November 13 @ 1:27 AM PST**

Full Moon in Gemini **November 27 @ 1:16 AM PST**

New Moon in Sagittarius **December 12 @ 3:31 PM PST**

Full Moon in Cancer **December 26 @ 4:32 PM PST**

2024 New & Full Moon Dates

New Moon in Capricorn **January 11 @ 3:57 AM PST**

Full Moon in Leo **January 25 @ 9:53 AM PST**

New Moon in Aquarius **February 9 @ 2:58 PM PST**

Full Moon in Virgo **February 24 @ 4:30 AM PST**

New Moon in Pisces **March 10 @ 1:00 AM PST**

Full Moon in Libra **March 25 @ 12:00 AM PDT**

New Moon in Aries **April 8 @ 11:20 AM PDT**

Full Moon in Scorpio **April 23 @ 4:48 PM PDT**

New Moon in Taurus **May 7 @ 8:21 PM PDT**

Full Moon in Sagittarius **May 23 @ 6:52 AM PDT**

New Moon in Gemini **June 6 @ 5:37 AM PDT**

Full Moon in Capricorn **June 21 @ 6:07 PM PDT**

New Moon in Cancer **July 5 @ 3:57 PM PDT**

Full Moon in Capricorn **July 21 @ 3:16 AM PDT**

New Moon in Leo **August 4 @ 4:12 AM PDT**

Full Moon in Aquarius **August 19 @ 11:25 AM PDT**

New Moon in Virgo **September 2 @ 6:55 PM PDT**

Full Moon in Pisces **September 17 @ 7:34 PM PDT**

New Moon in Libra **October 2 @ 11:49 AM PDT**

Full Moon in Aries **October 17 @ 4:26 AM PDT**

New Moon in Scorpio **November 1 @ 5:46 AM PDT**

Full Moon in Taurus **November 15 @ 1:28 PM PST**

New Moon in Sagittarius **November 30 @ 10:21 PM PST**

Full Moon in Gemini **December 15 @ 1:01 AM PST**

New Moon in Capricorn **December 30 @ 2:26 PM PST**

moon wisdom club

Sync with the moon & celebrate the many phases of life

JOIN US FOR MONTHLY ASTROLOGICAL
FORECASTS, RITUAL GUIDANCE, AUDIO
MEDITATIONS, YOGA SEQUENCES & MORE AT:

moonwisdom.com
@moonwisdomclub

Oracles to Guide You

THE SACRED CYCLES ORACLE

Deepen your relationship with the Moon cycle, your body, and the rhythms of Earth's Sacred Cycles.

THE SACRED SELF-CARE ORACLE

Find inspiration for creating self-care rituals that will nourish your mind, body, and spirit.

Find these and many other oracle decks in the Goddess Provisions Boutique at:

GODDESSPROVISIONS.COM/BOUTIQUE

Make   Magic

About the Authors

JILL PYLE, CO-FOUNDER OF GODDESS PROVISIONS

Jill is co-founder of Goddess Provisions (goddessprovisions.com), a community that provides resources and tools for people looking to connect with their divine feminine nature, deepen their spiritual practice, and journey within. Through cosmic downloads, she is guided to create offerings that help raise the vibration of the planet and push the consciousness evolution movement forward. Jill is also the author of *The Sacred Self-Care Oracle* and *The Sacred Cycles Oracle*.

EM DEWEY, CREATOR OF GARDEN OF THE MOON

Em is the creator of Garden of the Moon (gardenofthemoon.co), where she offers menstrual cycle support and education. She creates herbal "Cycle Support Kits" and digital resources for folks craving a more positive relationship with their periods. Em is passionate about working with the lunar calendar, cycle tracking, and teaching people how to use their body as a compass so they can reconnect with their innate wisdom. Em is a certified herbalist and holistic health coach, as well as the co-author of The Sacred Cycles Oracle.

CIDNEY BACHERT, COPYWRITER AT GODDESS PROVISIONS

Cidney is the copywriter and project assistant at Goddess Provisions. She is a creator, wordsmith, and advocate for access to holistic care. Through the written word, she hopes to inspire others to learn more about their bodies and the magic that everyone can produce. She is passionate about helping others find their zest for life while also developing a healthy and healing relationship with their inner cycles. Cidney is also a certified yoga instructor and Reiki practitioner.

JESSIE WHITE, ILLUSTRATOR AT SEEDS OF SPELLS

Jessie, also known as Jayanti, is an artist based in Canada who creates unique illustrations that act as a prayer, planting seeds and spells to bring healing to our planet. Her work, which is displayed at @seedsofspells on Instagram, is incredibly diverse and inclusive, portraying women in a variety of shapes, sizes, and colors to show the broad spectrum of the feminine vessel.

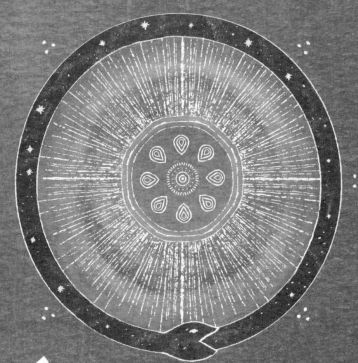

Embrace Your

Infinite Nature

We hope you enjoyed this Hay House book. If you'd like to receive our online catalog featuring additional information on Hay House books and products, or if you'd like to find out more about the Hay Foundation, please contact:

Hay House, Inc., P.O. Box 5100, Carlsbad, CA 92018-5100
(760) 431-7695 or (800) 654-5126
(760) 431-6948 (fax) or (800) 650-5115 (fax)
www.hayhouse.com® • www.hayfoundation.org

———

Published in Australia by: Hay House Australia Pty. Ltd.,
18/36 Ralph St., Alexandria NSW 2015
Phone: 612-9669-4299 • *Fax:* 612-9669-4144
www.hayhouse.com.au

Published in the United Kingdom by: Hay House UK, Ltd.,
The Sixth Floor, Watson House, 54 Baker Street, London W1U 7BU
Phone: +44 (0)20 3927 7290 • *Fax:* +44 (0)20 3927 7291
www.hayhouse.co.uk

Published in India by: Hay House Publishers India,
Muskaan Complex, Plot No. 3, B-2, Vasant Kunj, New Delhi 110 070
Phone: 91-11-4176-1620 • *Fax:* 91-11-4176-1630
www.hayhouse.co.in

———

Access New Knowledge.
Anytime. Anywhere.

Learn and evolve at your own pace
with the world's leading experts.

www.havhouseU.com